# Renaissance

Author      Linda Milliken
Illustrator    John Carrozza

EP167 ©Highsmith LLC 2000, 2003, 2007
4810 Forest Run Road
Madison, WI 53704

# Table of Contents

The Hands-on Heritage series has been designed to help you bring culture to life in your classroom! Look for the "For the Teacher" headings to find information to help you prepare for activities. Simply block out these sections when reproducing pages for student use.

# About the Renaissance

Renaissance (French for "rebirth") is the name historians have given to the time of great change that took place in Europe, mainly during the fifteenth and sixteenth centuries. Beginning in the fourteenth century, the people of Europe began to depart from the patterns of medieval life, which were still dominated by the power of the Roman Catholic Church. Scholarship and education were very limited. People did not move beyond the circle of their daily lives, and did not travel or explore.

The Renaissance really marks the beginning of humans' entrance into the industrial world. It was a time of tremendous growth and expansion of all aspects of life, including the arts, scholarship, and exploration.

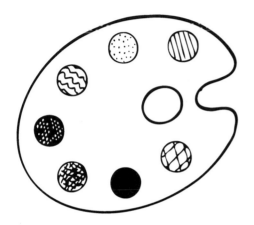

## Classical Models

The changes that marked the Renaissance began with artists and scholars when they discovered the art and history of the ancient Greeks and Romans. Ancient art placed more emphasis on human beings than on gods. Renaissance artists began to shift their attention away from religious to non-religious subjects. They copied the Greeks and Romans in trying to make people look as lifelike as possible. These changes led to the development of new paints and methods being used for art.

## Humanism

At the same time that artists were studying the ancient world, scholars were reading the history of the same period. Ideas about politics and society from the Roman past were new to Renaissance scholars. Their studies led them to question the whole system of ideas upon which their society was based. Gradually, their studies led them to a new thought system, called "Humanism," which says that the laws and systems of the world are made by humans, and they can be changed by humans. Humanism was concerned with education and the effect it could have on individuals by providing the key to true freedom.

## Science

As people began to accept the idea that they could make changes in the world, they became more curious about the world around them. Many advances were made in science during this period, especially in astronomy, physics, and medicine. Scholars began to develop a "scientific method"—a logical approach to asking and answering questions about the natural world. Scientific changes led to changes in technology. The invention of the printing press in the fifteenth century opened the world of science and ideas to people who never before had access to the written word.

# About the Renaissance

## Exploration

There were technological advances in the world of navigation. As people became more aware of the world around them, they began to want to explore it. In an effort to find better, less expensive trade routes, Europeans took to the sea. The Portuguese explored the possibilities of sailing around Africa to reach India and China. Christopher Columbus attempted to reach China by sailing west, and explored the New World. Improved instruments, such as the magnetic compass, and better map-making methods made this kind of exploration possible.

## Rationalism

When explorers brought back wealth and treasures from the New World, other changes began to take place in Europe. Trade routes across the Atlantic began to be more important than Mediterranean trade routes, which meant that Italy was losing its importance as a trade center. The countries that are now England, France, Germany, Austria, Switzerland, and Holland began to grow wealthier. Each nation began to develop a "national identity," and became more confident and active in world affairs.

## Religion

As nations emerged, the influence of the Roman Catholic Church began to decline. People began to question many of the basic beliefs of the church, and saw a need for reform in the Church. People in parts of Europe began to protest against what they felt were abuses by the Church and the reformers. This unrest led to civil wars and other types of social upheavals. The end result was a major change in the status of nations and their influence in the world.

## Towns & Cities

Throughout this period, the population of Europe was expanding. This led to the growth of cities and towns. People began to move from farms into the towns where work was available. The economy began to change in order to support the non-farming population, which led to changes in industry. The towns represented new wealth that was seen in merchants who made their living from the riches brought from the new trade routes. The wealthy merchants spent money on art and new buildings, and encouraged the growth of printing and research. They also financed many of the voyages of exploration.

EP167 Renaissance © Highsmith LLC 2007

# Humanism

During the Renaissance, scholars began to emphasize the importance of the individual. All things concerning humans and their lives on Earth became important. People took pride in their accomplishments and began to judge others on merit rather than on birth. The class into which a person was born did not influence his or her ability to accomplish deeds that were recognized by religious leaders and members of royalty.

This emphasis on humans formed a philosophy known as "humanism." To the Renaissance humanist, education meant the training of the "universal man," a person skilled in many fields of knowledge, including art, science, sports, and politics.

## Project

Create poster collages featuring individual skills and accomplishments.

## Materials

- poster board
- magazines
- scissors
- photographs
- glue, felt-tipped markers
- samples of papers, awards, or other memorabilia reflecting personal accomplishments

## Directions

1. Discuss the meaning of skill or accomplishment. Remember that a skill may be something like baking a batch of tasty cookies, or winning a trophy for outstanding athletic ability.

2. Gather photos, awards, or any other items that reflect your individual accomplishments. Assemble the items on poster board. Pictures cut from magazines or creatively lettered words may add to the project. Glue everything in place on the poster board to create a collage.

# People of the Age

The European people who lived during the Renaissance were constantly confronted by illness and disease. Half of the babies born died before their first birthday. Anyone who lived to be 40 years of age was thought to be very old. Women were kept under strict control by their fathers or husbands. Children were treated as adults, in both work and play.

There were distinct social classes who lived in completely different worlds. The wealthy ate fantastic meals, wore gorgeous clothes, and lived in beautiful homes. They had to pay few taxes and could buy their children a good education. There were far more poor people than wealthy people. The poor often went hungry. They wore simple, homemade clothing, which they rarely changed. They lived in shacks, which they often shared with their animals. They had little money, but paid most of the taxes. Most could not read, write, or afford an education.

## Project
Make stand-up paper models of Renaissance people.

## Materials
- Paper Models
- scissors
- crayons
- glue
- lightweight cardboard

## Directions
1. Use crayons to color each model.
2. Cut out the models. Place each model over lightweight cardboard and glue.
3. Cut out each model from the cardboard
4. Cut and trace the triangular shape on cardboard for each model. Cut out cardboard triangles. Fold on the dotted line and glue to the back of each model so it will stand.

## For the Teacher
Copy Paper Models (pages 7–8) for each student.

# Paper Models

Lady

Lord

Peasant Man

Peasant Woman

**Paper Models**

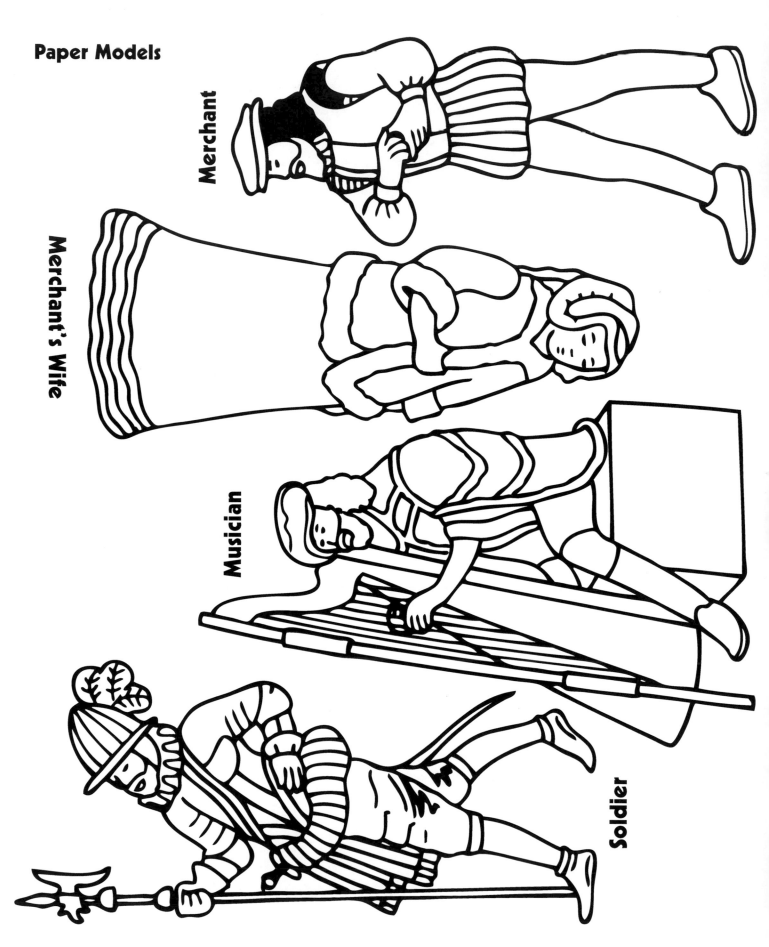

Merchant

Merchant's Wife

Musician

Soldier

EP167 Renaissance © Highsmith LLC 2007

# Trading

During the sixteenth century, profits from worldwide trade could be huge. Nobles hated the merchants who became rich from trading. They believed that inherited wealth was more honest than earned wealth. The rulers felt differently. Many emperors, kings, and queens borrowed money from the great merchant families. Merchants often grouped together to create trade companies, which were granted royal "monopolies." The grant allowed only one company to trade in certain goods or within a certain region.

Coins were important for international trade. Many were hammered by hand by craftsmen called minters. After 1550, more and more European coins were pressed by machine. Each coin had its own distinctive markings representing its country of origin. Each also had its own name. Some examples are the sovereign from England, piece of eight from Spain, the French teston, and thaler from Austria.

## Project

Design a unique coin for trading.

## Materials

- lightweight cardboard cut in circles of varying sizes
- aluminum foil, gift wrap
- markers
- scissors
- glue
- poster board
- zip-lock bags

## Directions

1. Use cardboard circles, aluminum foil, gift wrap, markers, and other craft materials to design a coin.

2. Make up to nine more coins to match. Mount one of each different coin to create a display.

3. Trade the remaining coins with classmates. Keep your coins in a zip-lock bag. Have them handy for trading.

# Craftsmen

Laborers skilled at their crafts worked with their apprentices to create the goods used by people all over Europe. Saddlers combined leather, woodwork, and metalwork to make saddles and bridles for horses. Blacksmiths forged iron into spurs and stirrups. Glassmakers made small bottles, tumblers, and window glass. Coopers made barrels for storing wine and salted meat. Clockmakers made astronomical clocks for the rich and privileged. Weavers worked in their cottages on huge wooden looms, spinning wool into warm cloth, which they dyed in huge tubs heated over fires.

Further refinements in glass and metalworking led to the development of many items that are in common use today. For the first time, items such as eyeglasses, scissors, buttons, and mirrors were improved upon and became more widely available.

## For the Teacher

### Project
Work in small groups to create Renaissance crafts.

### Materials
- Craft Cards
- as needed for each craft

### Directions
1. Discuss goods that were made during the Renaissance.
2. Make copies of the Craft Cards on page 11 so there is one task per student.
3. Cut the cards apart and distribute them among the students. Be sure they each work on a craft that is his or her "specialty."
4. Divide into small work groups, represented by the craft each student has selected.

# Craft Cards

## Brewer

*Many people in northern Europe brewed beer. In England, a license was needed to sell it.*

### Craft

Create a recipe for a special drink, then mix a batch to share with friends.

## Shipwright

*Shipwrights designed the galleons that took European explorers across the oceans to trade with new lands.*

### Craft

Build a model ship, or use pen and ink to create the drawings for one.

## Glassmaker

*Beautiful blown glass was made all over Europe, but Italians were known as the best glassmakers.*

### Craft

Use permanent markers to turn plastic glasses into a decorated set.

## Carpenter

*Carpenters made furniture and other household goods. Carpenters worked with masons and thatchers to construct houses.*

### Craft

Make bookends or another project from wood.

# Explorers

Little was known in the fifteenth century about the world outside Europe. This changed as Renaissance people became fascinated with unknown lands. In 1419, Prince Henry of Portugal made the first great voyage of what became known as the "Age of Exploration" when he explored the west coast of Africa.

Other daring voyages followed. Christopher Columbus, commissioned by the Spanish king and queen, sailed across the Atlantic in hopes of finding the East Indies. Italian navigator Amerigo Vespucci was the first to realize that the Americas were the new world and not part of China. Ferdinand Magellan was credited with making the first voyage around the world. Spain sent Hernando Cortés to Mexico, where he and his crew encountered the mighty Aztec Empire.

Explorers were given titles and other rewards for the riches they brought back from their voyages. New foods that were introduced included pineapples, sweet potatoes, cloves, and other spices. Hanging beds called "hamacas," now known as hammocks, were brought from the West Indies. Abundant amounts of gold and silver were melted and made into coins. All these things increased the wealth of the European countries that had commissioned the explorations.

## Project
Create an exhibit of New World discoveries.

## Materials
- table
- various art supplies
- student supplied objects
- resource materials

## Directions
1. Use resource materials to compile a list of things brought back to Europe by Renaissance explorers.
2. Create a tabletop exhibit. Bring real examples from home or make replicas using an assortment of art supplies.

# Galileo

Galileo Galilei was born in Pisa, Italy, on February 15, 1564. He has been called the founder of modern experimental science. As a child he showed skill in building toys. He made his first important scientific contribution at the age of 17. He discovered the laws of the pendulum, while watching a large lamp swing from the ceiling of a cathedral in Pisa. He timed the motions of the lamp with his pulse beat, noticing that each swing took the same amount of time, whether the arc was large or small.

He made the first practical use of the telescope to discover many new facts about the science of astronomy. He observed that the moon was not a smooth sphere, but that its surface was marked by valleys and mountains. He also observed that the Milky Way was a mass of stars "so numerous as to be almost beyond belief."

## Project

Paint the Milky Way as Galileo may have seen it through his telescope.

## Materials

- newspaper
- white construction paper
- blue, white, and yellow tempera paint
- toothbrush
- paintbrush

## Directions

1. Cover a table with newspaper to work on.
2. Cover your construction paper with a thin coat of blue tempera paint.
2. Use the toothbrush to spatter white and yellow tempera paint over the blue background.
3. Use fingertips and toothpicks to create swirls in the Milky Way.

# Engraving

Many printmaking techniques were in use during the Renaissance due to the printing press and the widespread availability of paper. Paper mills were not uncommon in Germany and Italy around 1390, when woodcuts were in wide use. Half a century later, a new technique was introduced by German artist Albrecht Dürer known as *intaglio* (cut or incised).

In this process, lines were cut into metal plates and the grooves were filled with ink. The surface was wiped clean, and then paper was pressed against the plate with enough pressure to force it to pick up the ink remaining in the grooves. There were three intaglio processes in use during the Renaissance: engraving, etching, and drypoint. The most popular of the three was engraving.

## Project
Make an engraving.

## Materials
- white construction paper
- scissors
- waxed paper
- ball-point pen
- black watercolor paint
- paintbrush

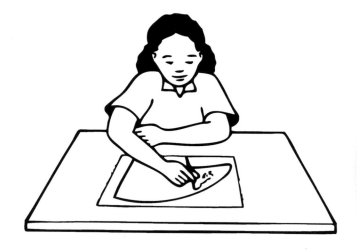

## Directions
1. Lay waxed paper, waxed side down, over the construction paper.

2. With a ball-point pen, engrave designs on the waxed paper, pressing hard enough to transfer the design to the construction paper below. Remove the waxed paper.

3. Brush a light coat of black paint over the design to make the engravings appear.

# Perfumed Oils

Careless personal hygiene was typical of Renaissance times. Rich and poor alike had little interest in bathing and rarely washed. Personal odors were sometimes covered with the use of perfumed oils. Even kings and the nobility had to use perfume to cover their body odor. The common people could not afford such luxuries. Soap was expensive and was not used as a routine part of hygiene, so stench was just an accepted fact of life. Poor hygiene and sanitary conditions led to the rampant spread of influenza, smallpox, and bubonic plague.

Dental hygiene was poor as well. People cleaned their teeth with mallow root or linen cloth. The rich often used ornate toothpicks. There were no toothbrushes.

## Project
Make a perfumed sachet.

## Materials
- inexpensive colognes or scented oils
- cotton balls
- fabric
- curling ribbon

## Directions
1. Cut the fabric into an 8-inch (20-cm) circle.
2. Spray several cotton balls with cologne. Place the cotton balls in the center of the fabric circle. Pull the sides of the fabric up and around the cotton balls. Tie the fabric with ribbon. Place in a drawer or desk.

# Language

Elizabethan language was very different from modern English. For example, the *o* sound was pronounced *uh* as in shove. The word ending *ed* was pronounced as a full extra syllable. The writings of William Shakespeare are cited most often in understanding Elizabethan speech.

People were well aware of their social standing in relation to the social standing of the person they were addressing. People wore clothing that identified their social standing, so knowing how to address them was easy. "Sir" or Mistress" was always appropriate for a person who was not nobility, but who was well-dressed. To children, "my lad" or "lass," or "good young sir" was appropriate.

## For the Teacher

### Project

Simulate a Renaissance conversation by employing historically correct words and phrases.

### Materials

- Language Chart
- examples of Shakespeare's plays

### Directions

1. Reproduce the Language Chart (page 17) for each student.
2. Practice some of the pronunciations with the class.
3. Read aloud some excerpts from Shakespeare's plays. Identify the language and phrases that sound different from modern English.
4. Try to integrate phrases and greetings into your daily conversation.

# Language Chart

## Pronunciation

- Want—*a* sounds like *apple*
- Make—sounds like *mek*
- Head—sounds like *haid*
- I—sounds like *uh-ee*
- Neither—sounds like *nayther*
- Lord—*o* sounds like the oo in *moon*
- Down—the *o* and *w* sound like *uh-oo*
- Surely—sounds like *sir-lee*
- Father—*a* sounds like *apple*; r sounds like a pirate: *Arrrr*

## Phrases

- He doth be
- Thou has
- Verily much
- Wherefore art thou?
- O'er there
- Take thy
- Aye Sir
- But nay!

**Never use one word where two will do! Add right, well, and most to your sentences.**

"He doth be most handsome."

"Thou art most busy."

## Greetings

### Children

- My lad/lass
- Good young sir
- My young lord/lady

### Officeholders (Judges, Knights)

- Your Honour
- Your Worship

### Commoners

- Wench (serving woman)
- Father (older man)
- Goodman, Goodwife

### Royalty (King or Queen)

- Your Highness
- Your Grace
- Her Majesty (when talking about the Queen)

### Nobility

- My Lord
- My Lord Earl
- My Lady
- My Lady Cousin

### Religious Leaders

- Sir Priest
- Master
- Brother, Sister

# Education

The amount of education Renaissance children received depended on their economic status. Poor children received very little education. They helped their parents with farm chores, spinning, and weaving. Country boys were usually first sent to school at the age of seven. They later became apprentices. Children of wealthy families were taught by a tutor as early as the age of two.

Most children did not have a book for their first lessons. They had a kind of wooden board with a handle, which was known as a hornbook. A piece of paper was stuck on one side. On the paper was written the alphabet, the numbers up to 10, and the Lord's Prayer. A thin sheet of transparent horn was placed over the paper to keep it clean. If they were successful in their lessons, they might be rewarded with a peppermint drop or gingerbread.

## Project

Make a hornbook.

## Materials

- Hornbook Pattern
- white paper
- cardboard
- scissors
- glue
- black markers
- peppermint candy

## Directions

1. Cut out the pattern. Use a black marker to write the alphabet, numbers to 10, and one nursery rhyme on the Hornbook Pattern.

3. Lay the pattern on a sturdier piece of cardboard and glue.

4. Cut the Hornbook out of the cardboard.

## For the Teacher

Copy one Hornbook Pattern (page 19) per student.

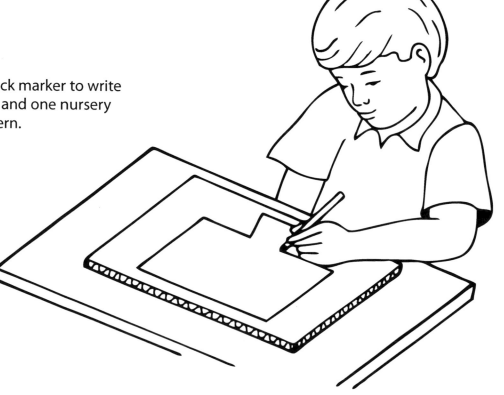

**Hornbook Pattern**

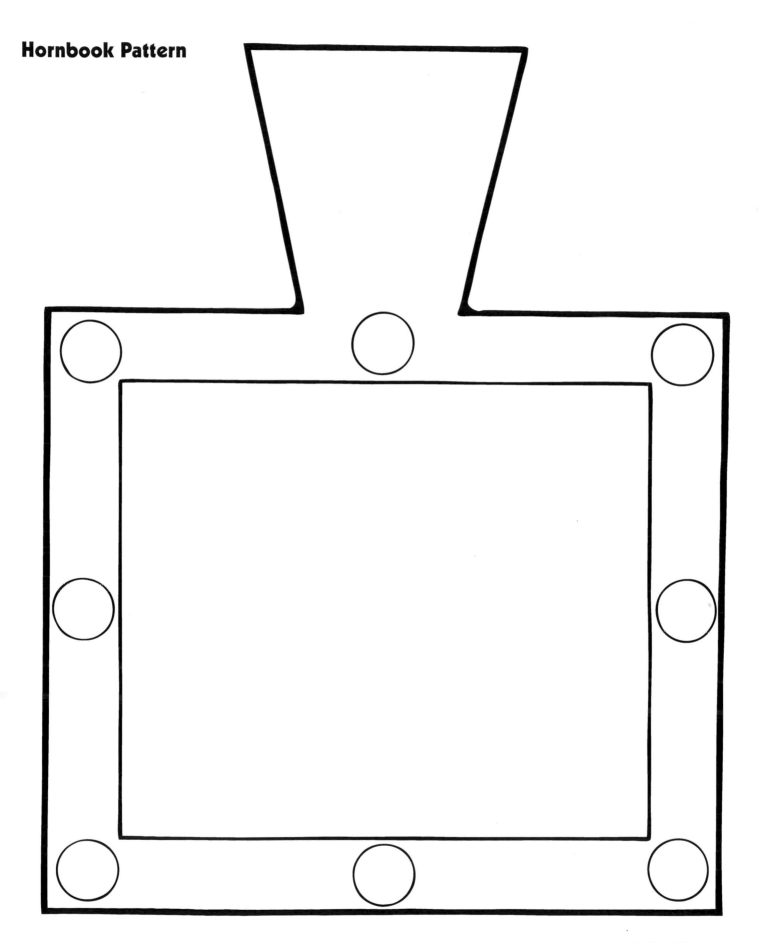

# Renaissance London

London was one of the largest cities in Europe during the Renaissance. London's main street was not a street at all, but the River Thames. It was bustling with traffic—fishing boats, barges, and merchant ships. Shallow rowing boats, called wherries, served as taxis and transported people from one section of town to another. Old London Bridge was the only bridge crossing the Thames. Carts, animals, and people were forced to squeeze between the high narrow buildings that jammed the bridge.

The center of life was St. Paul's, a magnificent Gothic cathedral. The cathedral was surrounded by narrow twisted streets, with overhanging house fronts. Sewage was just dumped in the streets. Beyond the city lay small villages with green fields and pastures where sheep and cattle grazed.

## Project

Paint a mural showing life in London and the River Thames.

## Materials

- paint
- paintbrushes
- white butcher paper

## Directions

1. Read the description of life in London, on the river Thames, and in the countryside surrounding the city.

2. In groups, paint various sections of the mural: London Bridge, the River Thames, St. Paul's Cathedral, the narrow streets of the city, and the countryside.

EP167 Renaissance © Highsmith LLC 2007

# Clothing

Clothing was often a direct indication of wealth. Peasants wore simple homespun clothing and woolen hats. For the wealthy, clothing was fancier and more complicated than ever before. Fabric was brightly colored, often with a design of large flowers. Outer garments were often slashed so that the fabric of garments worn underneath could be pulled through in small puffs. Women wore underskirts and outer skirts.

During the 1500s, both men and women wore fancy starched collars called ruffs. Men wore doublets, rich jackets of velvet or satin with puffed sleeves. Padded breeches had stockings sewn into the bottom. Children were dressed as infants only until the age of three, then they dressed the same as adults.

## Project
Dress in the style of the Renaissance.

## Directions
Use the descriptions below to bring costumes from home to wear with headwear and accessories.

## Unisex items (worn by women, men, and children)
- Shirt—off-white or dyed, often with full-bodied sleeves
- Cape—fabric draped over the shoulder, reaching to the small of the back
- Cloak—like a cape, only hooded and reaching to the ankles

## Women's Clothing
- Bodice—a type of laced vest worn over the shirt
- Skirts—two layers, an overskirt and an underskirt
- Snood—a loosely woven hair net

## Men's Clothing
- Breeches—pants without pockets
- Jerkin—a vest, belted at the waist and hanging to mid-thigh
- Slops—baggy trousers, usually cut to mid thigh
- Hose—knitted stockings worn under slops

## For the Teacher
Reproduce the Headwear and Accessories (pages 22–23) Project Pages for each student.

## Materials
- Headwear Project Page
- Accessories Project Page
- materials for projects

# Headwear Project Page

## Hennin

Women of wealth wore elaborate head coverings. The Hennin was a high, cone-shaped headdress worn during the late 1400s. It rose 3 to 4 feet (.9 to 1.2 m) high and was draped with a veil.

### Materials

- large sheet of poster board
- tape
- chiffon or other lightweight fabric
- stapler
- scissors

### Directions

1. Roll the poster board to form a cone sized to fit the head. Tape the sides together. Trim the bottom, if necessary.
2. Gather the fabric at one end and tape or staple it to the cone.

## Muffin Cap

The Muffin Cap was worn by men and women of the peasant or middle class. It was a loose cap with a floppy top. Sometimes a straw hat was worn over it.

### Materials

- white tissue paper
- white construction paper
- scissors
- tape

### Directions

1. Cut a construction paper band 2 inches (5.08 cm) wide and long enough to fit around the head, from the top of the fore-head and behind the ears. Tape the ends of the band together.
2. Cut a tissue paper circle, 2 feet (61 cm) in diameter.
3. Tape the tissue circle to fit around the band. You will need to make small folds or gathers along the outer edges.

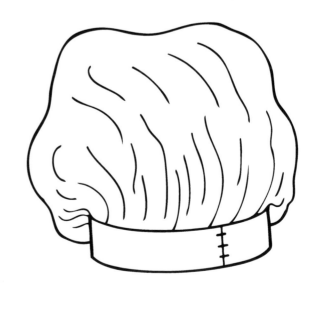

# Accessories Project Page

## Braided Belt

A common accessory worn by men and women was a loose-fitting braided belt with loops, on which were hung a variety of personal items. These might include keys, a knife, a leather pouch for coins, and a small cloth sack for other personal needs. Also hung on the belt was a tankard—a wooden or pewter drinking cup.

## Project

Make a braided belt and accessories.

## Materials

- thick yarn
- small paper bags
- scissors
- felt
- safety pins
- zip-lock bags
- cardboard
- personal items
- lightweight mug

## Directions

1. Braid three lengths of yarn to reach a length long enough to tie loosely around your hips.

2. Cut felt pieces about 2 x 4 inches (5 x 10 cm). Loop the felt pieces around the belt and secure them with safety pins.

3. Cut key shapes from cardboard and make pouches and small purses from zip-lock and paper bags. Cut slots in them so they can be strung on the belt or held by a loop. Fill the pouch with coins (see page 9).

4. Bring a lightweight plastic mug from home to string onto the belt. Add other personal items of choice.

# Needlework

Girls in wealthy families learned from their mothers how to spin, weave, and do fine needlework. Most learned how to embroider. Women's skirts were often open in front to show an embroidered slip (kirtle) underneath. Ornately embroidered curtains that could be closed for privacy hung around beds. Bedspreads were embroidered to match. Royal robes were adorned with elaborate embroidered patterns.

Embroiderers looked to nature for inspiration. Acorns and flowers were popular stitchery subjects. Intricate, abstract patterns were also created. English embroidery of the Elizabethan period was considered to be the finest in Europe.

## Project
Create a pattern on cloth using simple embroidery stitches.

## Materials
- Embroidery Stitch Chart
- embroidery floss
- embroidery needles
- solid color fabrics
- scissors

## Directions
1. Using the chart, practice the stitches on fabric scraps.
2. After you've practiced, use a variety of stitches to create a design on a 6-inch (15-cm) fabric square.

## For the Teacher
Copy one Embroidery Stitch Chart (page 25) per student. Cut fabric pieces into 6-inch (15-cm) squares. Save scraps for practice.

# Embroidery Stitch Chart

**Outline Stitch**

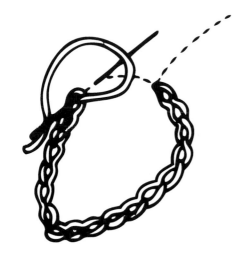

**Chain Stitch**

**Stroke Stitch**

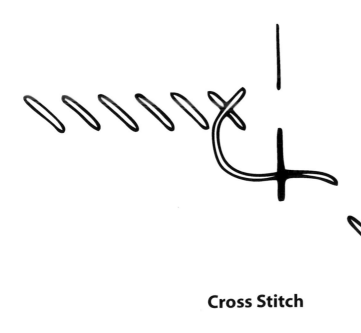

**Cross Stitch**

# Artists

Some of the greatest achievements of the Renaissance came in the arts. Renaissance artists invented new techniques in an effort to make their works as beautiful and lifelike as those of the ancient masters of Greece and Rome.

In Italy, artists searched for new styles to express the new ideas of the Renaissace. The beginning of the Italian Renaissance is usually linked with the painter Giotto, who painted in the 1300s. In the 1400s, new ways of mixing paint enabled artists to combine perspective with decorative styles. Sculptors such as Donatello and Michelangelo worked with bronze and glazed terra cotta. German artists developed the technique of oil painting. French kings and noblemen hired Italian artists to serve in their courts. Artistic achievements reached their height in the late 1500s, a period known as the High Renaissance.

## Project
Paint using the techniques of great Renaissance artist.

## For the Teacher
Copy pages 26, 27, and 28 for each student.

## Giotto

Giotto was born in Italy around 1267. He changed the decorative style of medieval painting by making his figures look like real men and women with human feelings. His best-known works are frescoes (wall paintings) of religious figures. He was also an architect and sculptor.

### Project
Create a fresco featuring everyone in class.

### Materials
- white butcher paper cut in 3-foot (1-m) wide sections
- tempera paint
- paintbrushes

### Directions
1. Sketch, then paint, a picture of yourself on the piece of butcher paper.
2. Tape the butcher paper sections end to end to create one long wall painting.

# Artist Project Page

## Masaccio

This early 1400s Italian painter worked out the laws of perspective to give his paintings an appearance of depth.

### Project

Draw a picture using the technique of perspective.

### Materials

- drawing paper
- crayons
- "P" volume of the encyclopedia

### Directions

- Look in the encyclopedia to find out more about techniques for drawing with perspective. Practice these techniques using crayons.

## Michelangelo

Michelangelo was born in Italy in 1475. A great painter, architect, and poet, he was mainly interested in creating large marble statues. He also is known for his ability to portray the human body in painting and sculpture. Michelangelo devoted most of his time to large projects. He spent four years painting the ceiling of the Sistine Chapel in the Vatican with frescoes depicting nine scenes from the Old Testament.

### Project

Create a "ceiling" painting.

### Materials

- butcher paper cut in sections the size of table tops
- markers
- tape

### Directions

1. Tape butcher paper to the underside of tables.
2. Lie underneath and use markers to create a "painting."

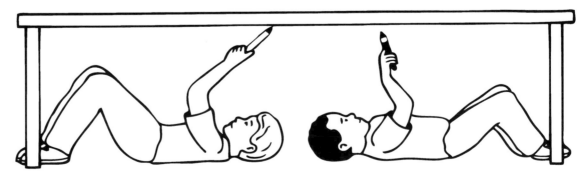

# Artist Project Page

## da Vinci

Leonardo da Vinci, an Italian artist of the late 1400s,
is best known for his paintings "Mona Lisa" and "The Last Supper."

### Project

Paint a portrait of a classmate.

### Materials

- tempera paints
- construction paper
- art books or encyclopedia featuring da Vinci's "Mona Lisa"

### Directions

Divide into pairs. Take turns posing for a portrait that shows classmates with the famous smile of Mona Lisa.

## Titian

Titian was born around 1487 in a town near Venice, Italy. He is known for his portraits of aristocrats and royalty, as well as for religious paintings. His use of bold brushstrokes and bright colors influenced European painting for more than 200 years.

### Project

Paint a portrait of a royal subject.

### Materials

- tempera paint
- tape
- wide-bristled paintbrushes
- butcher paper
- drop cloths or other floor protectors

### Directions

1. Cut a large piece of butcher paper for each artist. Tape the paper to the wall.
2. Use the techniques of Titian—large brushstrokes and bright colors—to paint a picture of a king or queen.

EP167 Renaissance © Highsmith LLC 2007

# Food

The peasants of the Renaissance period had a very different diet from the wealthy. Most could afford little more than coarse bread made from wheat, barley, or rye.

Sometimes the bread was stirred into a watery vegetable stew. Meat was too expensive for most people to buy. People in southern Europe ate fruit, although most people thought that fruit caused fevers.

Wealthier people had a richer and more varied diet. They ate meats and fish of all kinds, some of it dried and salted. Except for cabbage, vegetables were not often eaten. Explorers returning from the New World introduced turkeys and chocolate. Sugar was a luxury, and when it was obtained, it was sprinkled on everything, including meat. Wine and beer were the normal beverages for mealtimes, even for breakfast.

In the houses of royalty and the nobility, huge banquets were given. It was during the Renaissance that people began to set aside special rooms for eating, and elaborate dishes were cooked for guests.

## For the Teacher

### Project
Hold a Renaissance banquet in your classroom.

### Materials
See individual recipes.

## Beef Soup (Serves 20)

### Ingredients
- 1 gallon (3.79 liters) water
- four to six small onions, peeled and chopped
- handful parsley, chopped
- 10 beef bouillon cubes
- 20 peppercorns
- 4½ cups (1 liter) apple juice
- one bay leaf
- ground ginger and balsamic vinegar to taste
- four to six carrots, chopped
- 2½ pounds (1.13 kg) beef, cubed

### Directions
1. Put all ingredients except apple juice, ginger, and balsamic vinegar in a large pot. Bring to a boil.
2. Lower the heat and add apple juice. Simmer for 30 minutes, then add ginger and balsamic vinegar.
3. Simmer until meat is tender, approximately three hours.

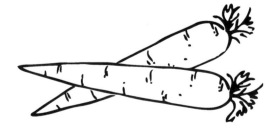

## Recipes

### Forced Eggs (Serves 20)

Forced eggs are very similar to the deviled eggs we eat today. Compare the taste of these eggs with deviled eggs from your favorite recipe!

#### Ingredients

- string or cheesecloth
- ⅓ cup (75 ml) each fresh basil and parsley
- ½ tsp. (2.5 ml) each powdered thyme and sage
- 2⅔ cups (630 ml) fresh bread crumbs
- 3 raw eggs
- ⅓ cup (75 ml) butter
- ¾ cup (180 ml) raisins
- ½ tsp. (2.5 ml) each pepper, cloves, and mace
- 1 tsp. (5 ml) each cinnamon and ginger
- 3 dozen hard-boiled eggs, cut in half and yolks removed (you will use 12 of the 36 yolks)

#### Directions

1. Combine the 12 reserved yolks with all remaining ingredients except the hard-boiled egg whites.
2. Lightly stuff each egg half with stuffing mixture. Place two egg halves together, stuffing to stuffing, and tie lightly with a string or a small strip of cheesecloth.
3. Place the eggs in a saucepan filled with lightly salted water. Boil gently five to 10 minutes to cook the stuffing, then serve.

### Celery

Celery was eaten after meals to aid digestion. It was also thought that celery had healing powers.

#### Ingredients

- celery
- salt
- pepper

#### Directions

1. Remove stalks from celery heart and wash carefully.
2. Serve with salt and pepper.

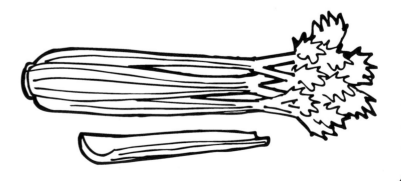

# Recipes

## Cabbage Salad (Makes 6 cups)

Cabbage was a staple in the Renaissance diet. It could be served raw or boiled in a stew or soup. This recipe is similar to cole slaw.

### Ingredients

- 1 small head of cabbage, grated
- ¾ cup (180 ml) cider vinegar
- 1½ Tbsp. (22 ml) sugar
- 1 tsp. (5 ml) salt
- 2 Tbsp. (30 ml) olive oil

### Directions

1. Remove the outer green leaves of the cabbage and discard them.
2. Grate the remaining cabbage.
3. Add oil and salt to the grated cabbage; mix well.
4. Mix the vinegar and the sugar. Add mixture to salad and stir.

## Strawberry Tarte (10–12 small servings)

Double-crust pies were popular because they could be eaten out of hand, without the need for utensils. Some pies were made of meat, but others were fruit pies.

### Ingredients

- 2 lbs (90 g) strawberries (frozen are okay)
- ⅓ cup (75 ml) sugar
- 1 tsp. (5 ml) cinnamon
- ½ tsp. (2.5 ml) cloves
- pastry for double-crust pie

### Directions

1. Preheat oven to 425° F (220° C).
2. Place bottom shell in pie pan. Cover bottom with half of the strawberries. Sprinkle berries with half of the sugar, cinnamon, and cloves.
3. Add the remaining berries and sprinkle with remaining dry ingredients.
4. Add top crust and bake for 45 minutes.

# Sculpture

Renaissance sculptors learned their craft by being apprenticed to working craftsmen. The apprentice learned skills such as the complicated procedure of sculpting in bronze. Unlike artists of previous ages, Renaissance sculptors carved figures that stood upright on their own and could be viewed from all sides. Some of the most magnificent Renaissance sculptures were produced in Italy. Famous sculptors of the age included Michelangelo, Donatello, Ghiberti, and Torrigiano.

Many Renaissance sculptors were commissioned by patrons (people who paid for the work). They were employed to create massive works such as tombs for important people, religious statues for cathedrals, and fountains for cities. Yet, not all sculpture was so grand in scale. Some sculptors were hired to make very small pieces like coats of arms for the fronts of town houses.

## Project

Work in cooperative groups to create a "marble sculpture" that can be viewed from all sides.

## Materials

- boxes of varying size
- white and black tempera paint
- sponges
- narrow-bristled paintbrushes
- masking tape

## Directions

1. In groups of four, stack and tape the boxes together to create a free-standing "sculpture."

2. Use white paint to sponge paint all surfaces. Create the effect of marble by painting black and gray lines over the sponge-painted surfaces. Use the sponge to blend the paints in some areas.

# Games

Board games like chess or backgammon were quite popular during the Elizabethan period. Children knew dozens of guessing games, often spending the hours after dinner asking each other riddles. Dice games were also popular.

Outdoor games were more rugged. Real tennis, a cross between modern tennis and squash, was played on special courts. Soccer was violent, played with a stuffed pig's bladder, teams of unlimited size, and no rules. Boys were permitted to play only the kind of games which would be useful to them in adult life. They were taught to fence, in the hope they would become good swordsmen. They learned jousting and tilting, which gave them practice in fighting on horseback with lances. Hunting and hawking were taught to prepare them to join family members in the field. They also practiced archery and fishing for recreation.

## Project
Play a variety of Renaissance games.

## Materials
See materials listed for each game or project on Games and Recreation Project Page (34).

## Checkers
Checkers was played on boards decorated with unique designs. Create a decorated checkerboard.

### Materials
- white construction paper square (at least 12 inches/31 cm square)
- checkers

### Directions
1. Fold the construction paper into 64 squares.
2. Use crayons to create two different patterns.
3. Color the squares using the two patterns to create a checker board.
4. Play a game of checkers.

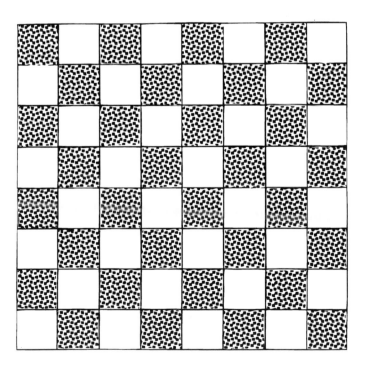

# Games and Recreation Project Page

## Trump

Children liked playing card games, especially one called Trump. Play a version of this card game.

### Materials

- deck of playing cards
- four players

### Directions

1. Shuffle and deal the cards face down.

2. Name one of the suits: diamonds, hearts, spades, or clubs.

3. Moving clockwise, each player takes a card from his pile and turns it face up on the table. When a card from the named suit appears, the first player to say "Trump" takes all the face-up cards on the table. Continue play.

4. When all cards are played, the player with the most cards is the winner. Name another suit and start a new game.

## Riddle Time

Many evening hours in country homes were spent playing guessing games.

### Materials

- books of guessing games and riddles
- large jar or other container
- index cards
- pencil

### Directions

1. Look through riddle books.

2. Each student chooses a riddle to write on an index card, remembering to memorize the answer.

3. Put all the riddles in a jar or container.

4. Each day, pull a riddle from the jar to challenge the class. The person who wrote it can verify the correct answer.

# Literature

Renaissance literature emphasized individual personality. New literature forms, such as essays and biographies, became important. By the sixteenth century, writers began to write in vernacular (native) languages, such as French and Italian instead of Latin, which had been used for writing during the medieval period.

Famous works by Italians included *The Prince* by Niccolò Machiavelli. Many leading French Renaissance writers lived and worked at the castles of the kings in the Loire Valley. They included poet Pierre de Ronsard and prose writer Françoise Rabelais. The English reached their highest accomplishments in drama, with playwrights William Shakespeare and Christopher Marlowe. Miguel de Cervantes of Spain wrote *Don Quixote*, which many critics have called the greatest novel ever written.

## Project
Write an autobiography.

## Materials
- writing paper
- pencil

## Directions
1. Discuss the elements of a biography. Then define autobiography.
2. Write an autobiography to display with your Humanism Collage. Try to use language and phrases characteristic of the Renaissance.

## For the Teacher
Use this activity in conjunction with the display of students' Humanism Collage (see page 5).

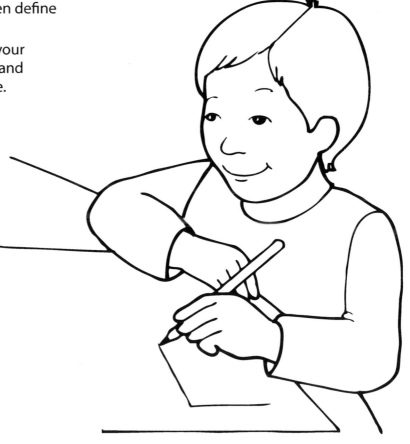

# Printing Press

Until the Renaissance, books were produced by hand, each individually copied and bound. Around 1450, the printing press was invented. Many historians agree that it was invented by Johannes Gutenberg of Germany. This printing press was combined with another invention—movable metal type. First, the individual letters of the alphabet were made in metal. The letters were then arranged into the words and sentences required for a page and clamped together in a frame. Once the page was printed, the type could be taken out, rearranged, and used again.

Early printed volumes were large and expensive. By the end of the fifteenth century, this changed. By that time, books came in a less expensive pocket size that people could carry around with them. More people had access to books, and literacy was on the rise.

## Project

Work in cooperative groups to create a printed page with "movable" type.

## Materials

- 2-inch (5cm) poster board block letters for tracing
- construction paper strips, 3 x 18 inches (8 x 46 cm)
- felt-tipped markers
- scissors
- sponges
- paper plates
- tempera paint

## Directions

1. Place the letter(s) on a sponge. Trace around the outline with a felt-tipped marker. Cut out the letters.

3. Dilute tempera paint slightly and pour it onto paper plates.

4. Work cooperatively to print words on the construction paper strips by dipping each sponge letter in the paint and pressing it gently to the paper.

5. Move around the classroom with your letter to help complete words. The students with vowels will be very busy! Create a word quilt on the classroom wall.

## For the Teacher

Give each student a block letter. Give two letters to the students who have little-used letters like *X* and *Z*. Double the vowels so that more than five students have them.

# Jewelry

Jewelry designs became very ornate during the Renaissance. Enamel, gems, and pearls were common decorations. Gemstones were often sewn directly onto garments and the richly decorated robes of monarchs.

Precious or semi-precious stones were set flat with a backing of metal. Earrings were considered an important item of a gentleman's costume. Elaborate chains and collars were worn by the wealthy and noble classes. Pendants were worn by both men and women. In the 1500s, a better method of cutting diamonds resulted in lighter and more graceful settings. This method of cutting produced diamonds that were shaped roughly like a rose, called rose diamonds.

## Project

Make a jeweled pendant.

## Materials

- cardboard
- tacky glue
- costume jewelry (available at thrift shops) or different colored sequins
- pin backs
- scissors
- ribbon

## Directions

1. Cut the cardboard into an oval or other shape suitable for a pendant.

2. Cut apart the costume jewelry or use sequins. Glue individual jewels onto the cardboard backing, covering the backing entirely.

3. When the glue has dried and the jewels have set, glue a a length of ribbon to the backside of the cardboard and hang around your neck.

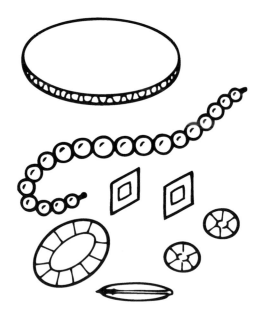

# Traveling Entertainers

Life in the country was hard. People worked from dawn until dusk to grow enough food to earn a meager living. During the work week there was little time for leisure. In spite of this hard work, people found time for many celebrations and festivals. There were celebrations for the harvest, Midsummer's Day, and May Day. Some festivals were reminders of ancient rites intended to ensure that the earth would stay fertile. They were also occasions for dancing, games, and other forms of recreation.

Contributing to the festivities were traveling entertainers, such as musicians, jugglers, puppeteers, and actors performing simple folk plays. These traveling entertainers were sometimes viewed as no better than beggars, but for the hard-working people of the country villages, they provided important amusement.

## Project

Make and use juggling sticks.

## Materials

- fabric cut into 4-inch (10.16 cm) strips
- ½-inch (1.25-cm) wooden dowels; 1 long and 2 short per student
- tape
- electrical tape
- rubber tape
- duct tape

## Directions

1. Wrap electrical tape in a spiral pattern around the dowel, leaving room between strips for the rubber tape to be wrapped as well.

2. Wrap rubber tape around the dowel, covering the bare strips left by the electrical tape.

3. Tape the fabric strips to form a fringe at the end of the dowel. Use duct tape to hold in place and form weight at the end of the sticks.

6. Wrap two-thirds of each of the smaller dowels with alternating electrical and rubber tape. Wrap the remaining one-third with electrical tape for hand holds.

7. Practice juggling and throwing the large juggling stick up in the air with the two shorter dowels.

# Shakespeare

William Shakespeare was an English playwright and poet. He was born in the small market town of Stratford-upon-Avon. He moved to London at an early age, and quickly established himself as one of the city's leading actors and playwrights.

Shakespeare wrote at least 37 plays, which have been divided into the categories of comedies, histories, and tragedies. Most of the plays were written for public theaters. When theaters closed due to the outbreak of the plague, Shakespeare turned to writing poems. Poetry was considered more honorable than plays by the people of the times.

There was no scenery in Renaissance plays. A play's setting was unknown until the characters identified it through their lines. Colorful costumes, sound effects, and props such as thrones, swords, banners, rocks, trees, and beds helped tell the story.

## For the Teacher

### Project
Create sound effects that may have been heard during a production of one of Shakespeare's plays.

### Materials
- drums, horns, and other musical instruments
- a variety of student-supplied objects to create sound effects
- chalkboard, chalk

### Directions
1. Brainstorm a list of things that may have needed sound effects in one of Shakespeare's plays. Write the list on the chalkboard. Here are some ideas to start: rain; horses' hooves; a duel; and the arrival of Her Majesty, the Queen.

2. Divide the list into equal parts and assign sections to class groups. Give each group the task of devising a way to create sound effects for each item on its list.

3. Have the groups create the sound effects for the rest of the class. Can students identify them?

# Theater

By the late 1500s, plays were performed in two types of theater buildings—smaller private theaters had candlelight for evening performances. Public theaters were larger, holding as many as 2,500 people. These theaters had no lighting, so performances were held during the day. Public theater buildings could be round, square, or many sided. They were built around a courtyard, called a pit, that had no roof. The theater consisted of three levels of galleries, and stood about 32 feet (10 m) high.

The stage was a large platform that extended into the pit. There were dressing rooms, wardrobe rooms, and an upper stage or balcony. Actors—men and boys, as women did not perform on the Elizabethan stage—performed on the main stage, in the "discovery" space, and on the upper stage. The audience stood in the pit or sat in the galleries. Music and sound effects were produced with machinery in a hut on top of the roof.

## Project
Construct a stand-up model of an Elizabethan public theater.

## Materials
- Theater Patterns
- crayons
- scissors
- poster board
- glue
- stapler

## Directions
1. Color the drawing. Cut out around the outlines.
2. Center the theater drawing on the poster board. Glue and cut out.
3. Cut the poster board into a 6 x 22-inch (15 x 55-cm) strip.
4. Glue or staple the ends of the strip to each side of the drawing to form a circle, as shown.
5. Add features inside the theater. Build miniature props and figures of actors.

## For the Teacher
Copy one Theater Pattern (page 41) per student.

**Theater Pattern**

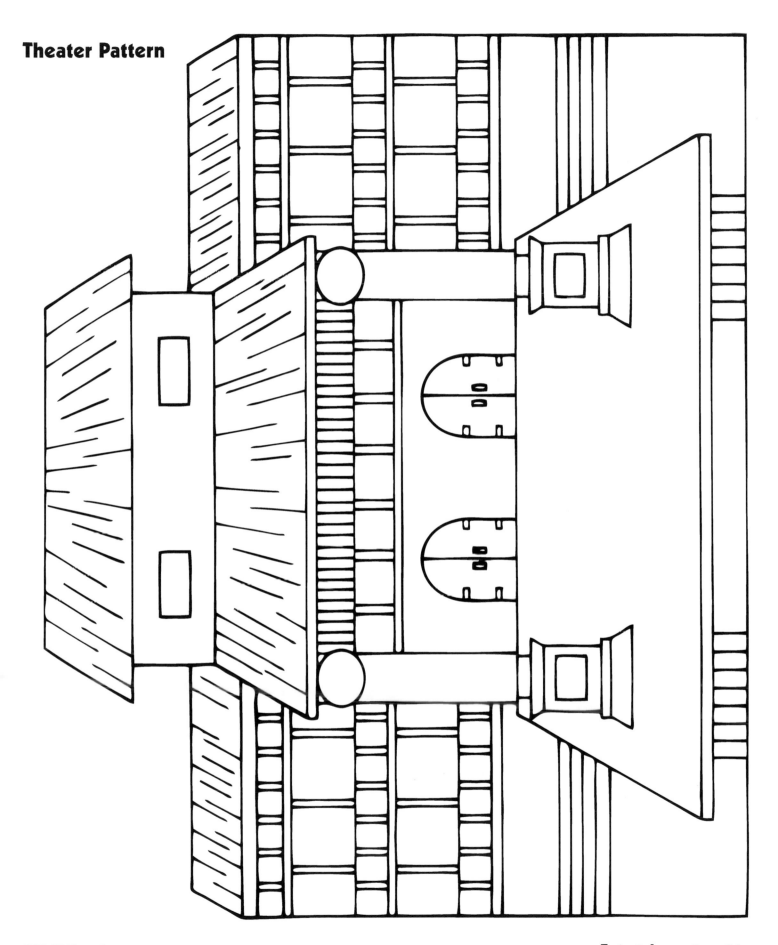

# Masque

A masque is a courtly form of dramatic entertainment named after the masks and elaborate costumes worn by the performers. It originated in England, where it was first called mummery. Over time, it developed into a folk play. Italy adopted it later as a court spectacle that included songs, dances, and scenery. From Italy it spread to France, then back to England during the early 1500s. Masques were given at court, with nobles and ladies taking parts.

The masques were simple performances, and generally lacked story, action, crisis, or ending. The performers recited long, poetic speeches. Ben Jonson was a noted writer of masques during the Renaissance. He introduced masques with two sets of performers and elaborate staging.

## Project
Make a mask for a performer in a masque.

## Materials
- variety of craft materials including construction paper, foil, ribbons, yarn, paper bags, trims, paper plates, tissue paper, etc.
- scissors
- glue

## Directions
1. Choose from an assortment of craft materials to design an original mask.

# Music

Renaissance composers did not have classical models for their music because the Greeks and Romans thought words more important than music. Most of the music that was written during the Renaissance was to accompany singing. Music was composed for religious services such as Mass or to accompany the singing of psalms.

Madrigals, songs for four to six voices singing in harmony and accompanied by instruments, were especially popular. These songs were secular and dealt with love and romance.

Musicians were employed to play at lavish balls, and theatrical performances. Traveling musicians roamed from village to town, entertaining at *faires*. Lutes were sometimes provided in barbershops for waiting gentlemen to play. Simple woodwind instruments, recorders, and small flutes were also commonly played. One of the most well-known songs from this period is "Greensleeves" believed to be written by Henry VIII. To play this music, new instruments like the violin and harpsichord were invented.

## For the Teacher

### Project
Learn music and lyrics of two Renaissance rounds.

### Materials
- Renaissance Song Lyrics (page 44)
- simple instruments like recorders, harmonicas, and rhythm instruments

### Directions
1. Reproduce the Renaissance Song Lyrics for each student.
2. Learn the tune to each song. Practice singing together, then divide into groups and try singing in rounds.
3. Choose a few students to accompany the singers with background music on recorders, harmonicas, shakers, and small drums.

# Rose, Rose

*This is a four-part round of English origin.*

Rose, rose, rose, rose, Will I ev - er see thee red?

Aye, mar - ry, that I will, If thou but stay.

# White Sand and Gray Sand

*This is a traditional English round*

White sand and gray sand; Who'll buy my white sand? Who'll buy my gray sand?

# Dancing

Dancing was an important part of a boy's or girl's education. Every wealthy family held dances at Christmas, weddings, and other festive occasions. In early Tudor times, the dances usually took place in the dining hall. Eventually most stately homes had a long gallery where dances could be held. One of the most popular dances was the galliard, a showcase dance for male dancers. It was a brisk, lively dance composed of a series of small running and leaping steps.

Folk dancing was popular among the commoners. One form, Morris dancing, was thought to bring luck. It was performed for Easter, May Day, and during spring planting to ensure a good crop. Morris dancers wore bright colors and tied as many as 40 scarves, ribbons, handkerchiefs, and bells around their legs.

## For the Teacher

### Project
Create a modern-day dance similar to the running and leaping steps of the galliard.

### Materials
- playground area
- cassette or CD player for each student group
- music, selected by students

## Directions

1. Divide the class into dancing groups of six members.
2. Each group discusses and decides on the choice of music for its dance. All songs should be approved by the teacher!
3. Head outside for some original choreography. Each group will create an original series of small running and leaping steps to perform to its music.

# May Day

Living and working in a town was hot and tiring. Only a few of the largest palaces had gardens. Many wealthy city dwellers built villas in the countryside where they went to rest, enjoy traveling faires, and participate in the festivities of traditional celebrations.

One important celebration took place on May Day. This festival began as a religious event, but it eventually became a harvest celebration. It centered around a Maypole, a tall tree trunk that had been chopped down, then decorated with garlands of flowers and herbs. Flags and ribbons were tied to the top, and there was dancing around the Maypole. Floral garlands were also shaped into simple headdresses and worn by peasants and other country ladies.

## Project

Create floral garlands to decorate the classroom or to make into a headdress.

## Materials

- green crepe paper
- tissue paper
- curling ribbon
- clear tape
- scissors
- string

## Directions

1. Cut crepe paper into 4-foot (1.2-m) lengths. Put two lengths together and secure them with tape at one end. Twine the two lengths together to create a rope effect.

2. Make tissue paper flowers by cutting circles, gathering them tightly in the center, and taping or tying the gathered end.

3. Tuck the flowers into the crepe paper garland. Wind ribbon through the crepe paper.

4. Drape the garland on classroom walls, doors, and desks. Or, form and tape a garland into a circular shape to create a headdress.

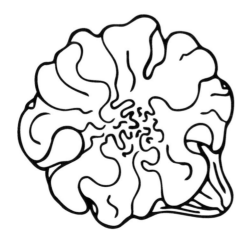

# Literature List

Check with your librarian for other titles about the Renaissance.

## Galileo: The Genius Who Faced the Inquisition
by Philip Steele. National Geographic, 2005. 64 p. Gr. 4–8
Biography of the father of modern science.

## Giants of Science: Leonardo da Vinci
by Kathleen Krull. Viking Juvenile, 2005. 128 p. Gr. 4–8
A lively biography of one of the most renowned artists (and painter, architect, inventor, and engineer) of the Renaissance.

## Johann Gutenberg and the Amazing Printing Press
by Bruce Koscielniak. Houghton Mifflin, 2003. 32 p. Gr. 2–6
A history of the modern printing industry, looking particularly at the printing press invented by Gutenberg around 1450 but also at its precursors.

## Leonardo and the Flying Boy
by Laurence Anholt. Barron's Educational Series, 2000. 32 p. Gr. 2–4
Short fictional account of Leonardo da Vinci through the eyes of his two apprentices.

## Leonardo, Beautiful Dreamer
by Robert Byrd. Dutton, 2003. 40 p. Gr. 3–7
Illustrations and text portray the life of Leonardo da Vinci, who gained fame as an artist through such works as "Mona Lisa," and as a scientist by studying various subjects including anatomy and flight.

## Life in the Renaissance: The City
by Kathryn Hinds. Benchmark Books, 2003. 95 p. Gr. 5–8
Describes city life during the Renaissance, from about 1400 to 1600, explaining how cities varied in government, commerce, population, and culture, and how they influenced the shaping of European civilization. Other titles in this attractive series include The Church, The Court, and The Countryside.

## Makers of the Middle Ages and Renaissance: Queen Elizabeth and England's Golden Age
by Samuel Willard Crompton. Chelsea House, 2005. 148 p. Gr. 4–7
Biography of the queen under whose rule literature, fashion, and education came to the forefront.

## Michelangelo
by Diane Stanley. HarperCollins, 2000. 48 p. Gr. 4–7
A biography of the Renaissance sculptor, painter, architect, and poet, well known for his work on the Sistine Chapel in Rome's St. Peter's Cathedral. Readers may also enjoy Stanley's other biographies of Renaissance notables: Leonardo Da Vinci, Good Queen Bess: The Story of Elizabeth I of England, and Bard of Avon: The Story of William Shakespeare.

## The Paint Box
by Maxine Trottier and Stella East. Fitzhenry and Whiteside, Ltd., 2004. 32 p. Gr. 1–4
Fact and fiction blend in this story about the daughter of Italian Renaissance painter Jacopo Tintoretto.

## Passport to History: Your Travel Guide to Renaissance Europe
by Nancy Day. Runestone Press, 2001. 96 p. Gr. 4–7
Takes readers on a journey back in time to experience life in Europe during the Renaissance, describing clothing, lodging, foods, local customs, transportation, notable personalities, and more.

## The Second Mrs. Giaconda
by E. L. Konigsburg. Aladdin reprint, 1998. Gr. 5–8
This art mystery of sorts relates how Leonardo da Vinci came to paint the "Mona Lisa," from the point of view of his servant Salai.

## Starry Messenger
by Peter Sís. Farrar, Straus and Giroux, 1996. 40 p. Gr. 1–6
Describes the life and work of Galileo Galilei, who changed the way people saw the galaxy by offering objective evidence that the earth was not the fixed center of the universe. Caldecott Honor Book.

# Glossary

**alchemy**—a semi-scientific study of chemistry limited to the search for the secret of transmutation, or changing one natural substance into another

**apothecaries**—people who made and sold herbal and other cures in their shops

**apprentice**—a boy who was sent to learn a particular trade or craft with a qualified trader or craftsman

**astrolabe**—an instrument for measuring the altitude of stars

**classical culture**—the art of learning of the ancient Greeks and Romans

**Elizabeth I**—Queen of England from 1558 to 1603

**Ferdinand Magellan**—the Portuguese sea-captain who led the first expedition to sail around the world, from 1519 to 1522

**Francisco Pizarro**—Spanish soldier who led a tiny army that conquered the vast empire of the Incas in Peru, from 1531 to 1533

**Galileo Galilei**—Italian scientist who discovered the law of the pendulum

**galliard**—a brisk, lively dance

**Hernando Cortés**—explorer who led a small Spanish expedition to Mexico in 1519; he had achieved the conquest of the entire Aztec Empire by 1521

**Humanists**—writers and scholars who were particularly interested in the learning of ancient Greece and Rome

**intaglio**—a method of printmaking, using the technique of cutting or incising, that included the processes of engraving, etching, and drypoint

**kirtle**—embroidered undergarment

**Leonardo da Vinci**—Italian artist and inventor who painted the "Mona Lisa." He spent much time at the court of Francis I of France, and died in 1519

**Martin Luther**—a German professor who complained bitterly about the corrupt Roman Catholic Church, then set up his Protestant church

**masque**—a spectacular court entertainment that included music, dancing, and acting

**master craftsman**—a craftsman who was especially skilled at his work; a master craftsman had to pass many tests to prove his skill

**muffin cap**—loose cap with floppy top worn by men and women

**navigation**—finding a way between different places; sailors navigated their ships by using charts and looking at the position of the stars

**perspective**—a method of drawing objects in such a way that they appear to have depth and distance

**philosopher**—someone whose work is to study and develop ideas about how people should live

**Protestants**—the name that came to be given to Christians who complained about the Roman Catholic Church and set up their own churches

**quadrant**—an instrument used to measure angles, used by both navigators and astronomers to measure the positions of the sun and stars

**Roman Catholic Church**—the only Christian Church in western Europe before the Protestants broke away

**scholar**—a person whose life is devoted to study and research

**spices**—pepper, cinnamon, cloves, etc., which came from the East and were used to season food

**wherries**—rowing boats that served as "taxis" in Renaissance London

**William Shakespeare**—an actor from Stratford-on-Avon in England; he became the best-known playwright in the English language

EP167 Renaissance © Highsmith LLC 2007